EXPLORING WORLD CULTURES

Hungary

Joanne Mattern

Cavendish Square

New York

Published in 2020 by Cavendish Square Publishing, LLC
243 5th Avenue, Suite 136, New York, NY 10016

Library of Congress Cataloging-in-Publication Data

Names: Mattern, Joanne, 1963- author.
Title: Hungary / Joanne Mattern.
Description: First edition. | New York : Cavendish Square, 2020. |
Series: Exploring world cultures | Includes bibliographical references and index. | Audience: Grades 2-5.
Identifiers: LCCN 2018050356 (print) | LCCN 2018056016 (ebook) | ISBN 9781502647290 (ebook) |
ISBN 9781502647283 (library bound) | ISBN 9781502647269 (pbk.) | ISBN 9781502647276 (6 pack)
Subjects: LCSH: Hungary--Juvenile literature.
Classification: LCC DB906 (ebook) | LCC DB906 .M377 2020 (print) |
DDC 943.9--dc23
LC record available at https://lccn.loc.gov/2018050356

Editorial Director: David McNamara
Editor: Lauren Miller
Copy Editor: Nathan Heidelberger
Associate Art Director: Alan Sliwinski
Designer: Christina Shults
Production Coordinator: Karol Szymczuk
Photo Research: J8 Media

The photographs in this book are used by permission and through the courtesy of:
Cover Sue Cunningham Photographic/Alamy Stock Photo; p. 5 Peter Wallace/Shutterstock.com; p. 6 pavalena/Shutterstock.com; p. 7 grafvision/Shutterstock.com; p. 8 Rolf Richardson/Alamy Stock Photo; p. 9 Universal Images Group/Getty Images; p. 10 Laszlo Balogh/Getty Images; p. 11 photo.ua/Shutterstock.com; p. 12 Bloomberg/Getty Images; p. 13 parlanteste/Shutterstock.com; p. 14 UrosPoteko/iStock/Getty Images; p. 15 Bernd Wolter/Shutterstock.com; p. 16 Marka/Universal Images Group/Getty Images; p. 18 Tupungato/Shutterstock.com; p. 19 FERENC ISZA/AFP/Getty Images; p. 20 richard sowersby/Alamy Stock Photo; p. 21 Christian Kober/AWL Images/Getty Images; p. 22 imageBROKER/Alamy Stock Photo; p. 24 Ixefra/Moment/Getty Images; p. 26 Melinda Nagy/Shutterstock.com; p. 27 ODD ANDERSEN/AFP/Getty Images; p. 28 Olesia Nosova/iStock/Getty Images; p. 29 Viktor1/Shutterstock.com.

Printed in the United States of America

Contents

Hungary is a country in eastern Europe. It has many different landscapes, including mountains, rivers, and lakes. There are also flat plains and thick forests, and even hidden caves! Hungary has both beautiful farms in the countryside and big, modern cities.

Hungary is surrounded by other countries. It does not border any oceans. However, the Danube River is an important waterway that runs through the middle of the country.

Almost ten million people live in Hungary. The nation has a long and interesting history. Hungary's people are friendly. They work hard, but they also enjoy sports and music. They celebrate holidays and eat delicious foods. Hungary is a fascinating and interesting nation to explore.

The Danube River flows through the city of Budapest, splitting it in two.

Geography

Hungary covers 35,919 square miles (93,030 square kilometers). Austria and Slovenia neighbor Hungary to the west. Croatia

This map shows Hungary and its neighbors.

and Serbia lie to the south. Romania is east of Hungary. Ukraine and Slovakia border Hungary to the north.

FACT!

Budapest was once two separate cities, named Buda and Pest. They became one city in 1873.

6

Under the Earth

There are hundreds of caves underneath northwestern Hungary. These caves are part of Aggtelek National Park. Thousands of people visit every year.

Inside the caves at Aggtelek National Park

The most important waterway in Hungary is the Danube River. It flows through the middle of Budapest, Hungary's capital city. There are mountains in the north and west. In the southeast, the Great Hungarian Plain stretches across almost half of the country. It is covered with grass and provides good land for farming. Many lakes and small rivers flow across this plain.

7

During the 800s CE, a group of tribes called the Magyars started ruling what is now Hungary. Their leader, Arpad, is called the **founder** of Hungary. In the year 1000, Arpad's great-great-grandson, Stephen, became the first king of Hungary.

A carving of Stephen, the first king of Hungary

Hungary became a large and powerful country. However, other countries took some of its land. During the 1800s, Hungary and

FACT!

In 2012, Hungary changed its name from the Republic of Hungary to just plain Hungary.

A Shrinking Nation

After World War I, Hungary shrank from 125,641 square miles (325,409 sq km) to its present size.

This map shows all the countries that once made up the empire of Austria-Hungary.

Austria joined to form the Austro-Hungarian Empire. The empire was destroyed during World War I. After the war, Hungary had to give up much of its land.

After World War II, Hungary became a **communist** country. Its government was supported by the Soviet Union. Communism lasted in Hungary until 1989. Then, Hungary became a **republic**.

VOTE ✓

Hungary is a parliamentary republic. Its government is split up into three parts: executive, legislative, and judicial.

A National Assembly meeting in May 2018

The president and the prime minister make up the executive part. The prime minister has the most power. He or she appoints people to lead different departments. The prime minister is elected to a four-year term.

FACT!

Hungary's national anthem is called "Himnusz." It became the national anthem in 1844.

Hungary's Capital

Budapest is the capital of Hungary. About 1.8 million people live there.

The National Assembly building is in Budapest.

The National Assembly makes up the legislative part. Each member is elected to a four-year term. The assembly has 199 members. Members of the National Assembly make new laws. They can also make decisions about war or other military actions.

The judicial branch enforces the law. The top court in Hungary is called the Curia. Smaller courts operate under the Curia. The Curia makes sure laws are carried out correctly.

The Economy

About 65 percent of Hungary's workers have jobs in service industries. Some of them work in hotels, restaurants, museums, and banks. Others work in hospitals and schools. Tourism is a big part of Hungary's economy.

Workers assemble a car in a Hungarian factory.

Manufacturing is also an important industry. Hungary's mines produce a mineral called bauxite.

FACT!

Hungarian farmers raise cows for their meat and their milk.

Hungarian money is called the forint. Forints are decorated with pictures of famous Hungarians.

A stack of colorful Hungarian forints

Bauxite is used to make aluminum. Other workers mine coal, oil, and natural gas. Factory workers make paper products, food, and chemicals.

Farming was once the largest part of Hungary's economy. In the past, farms were owned by the government. Today, farms are owned by Hungarian citizens. Only about 5 percent of Hungary's workers have jobs on farms. Wheat, corn, potatoes, beets, and sunflower seeds are the top crops.

Hungary is a mix of plains, mountains, and water. Major rivers, like the Danube and Tisza, are home to fish, turtles, and beavers. The country's lakes also have these animals. Birds such as ducks, geese, and swans swim there too.

Roe deer are common across Europe.

A variety of animals live in Hungary's forests and fields. Large animals like wild boars and red

FACT!

Thousands of cranes fly through Hungary every autumn. They are on their way to Africa for the winter.

14

Beautiful Butterflies

Hungary is home to 150 kinds of butterflies. Some are common in Hungary but rare in other parts of Europe.

A purple emperor butterfly enjoys the sun on a warm Hungarian day.

deer live in the forests. Wolves, bears, and jackals live there too. Herds of deer also roam across the plains.

About 20 percent of the land is covered with forests. Beech, oak, poplar, and willow trees are the most common. Beautiful flowers like peonies, daisies, and tulips bloom in fields and gardens.

15

Almost all Hungarians are natives. Their ancestors are the Magyars who ruled long ago.

There are other **ethnic** groups in Hungary. The largest is the Roma. The Roma

Children wear traditional clothes during a festival in Kalocza, Hungary.

FACT!

Hungary's population has been getting smaller every year. Fewer babies are being born, and many Hungarians are moving to other countries for work.

The Roma

The Roma have been treated badly for hundreds of years. Today, the government is working to make laws more fair and helpful.

are sometimes called Gypsies. The Roma once traveled the land in horse-drawn wagons. They were nomads. This means they never stayed in one place for long. Today, they have settled in most of Hungary's towns and cities.

There are also small groups of Germans, Serbs, Slovaks, and Romanians. Many of these people moved to Hungary after World War II to escape the violence in their own countries. They came looking for safety and opportunities for a better life.

Lifestyle

Most Hungarians live in cities or large towns. The capital, Budapest, is also the largest city in Hungary. Other large cities include Debrecen, Pecs, and Gyor. Here, most people live in apartments.

Budapest's streets and cafés are always busy.

Other parts of Hungary are filled with small villages. There, people live in small houses with tiled roofs. Many villagers grow vegetables and

FACT!

The University of Pecs was founded in 1367. It is the oldest university in Hungary.

fruit in large gardens. There is a lot of green space. People from the city like to visit the countryside on weekends and holidays.

Hungarian children start school when they are six years old. They go to primary schools until they are fourteen. Students learn Hungarian, math, science, and foreign languages.

After Primary School

When they are fourteen, Hungarians go to secondary school. Here, they get ready to go to college or learn a **trade.** Students must pass a difficult exam to go to college.

Students in a Hungarian classroom

Religion

People in Hungary can choose to follow any religion. Most Hungarians are Christian. About one-third of Hungarians belong to the Roman Catholic Church. Other Hungarian Christians belong to Protestant churches.

Saint Stephen's Basilica is the largest church in Budapest.

Judaism is another important religion in Hungary. Before World War II, about nine hundred thousand Jews lived in Hungary. However, they

Many Hungarians do not follow any religion.

A Huge Church

The Esztergom Basilica is the tallest building in Hungary and the most important Catholic church in the country.

The Esztergom Basilica was built in 1856.

were **persecuted** and faced unfair laws. In 1991, Hungary passed new laws to help Jewish people and communities. Today, there are about fifty thousand Jewish people in Hungary. The Great Synagogue in Budapest is the largest synagogue in the nation.

Language

Almost everyone in Hungary speaks Hungarian. This language's official name is Magyar. It originally came from the area around Finland and Russia, in northern Europe and Asia.

Most newspapers are written in Hungarian. There are a few in other languages, including English.

FACT!

In Hungarian, the words in a sentence can be put in a different order to explain things better.

How Do You Say That?

Hungarian is not an easy language to learn. However, some simple words to say include "thank you" and "you're welcome." "Thank you" is *köszönöm* (KUH-suh-num), and "you're welcome" is *szívesen* (SEE-vah-shen).

Hungarian is a very hard language to learn. It has forty-four letters. There are fourteen vowels that can change the meaning of a word depending on how they are pronounced. There are many different rules to follow as well.

People in Hungary speak other languages too. Many people speak English or German. Others speak Russian or French. Students can study these languages in school.

Christmas and Easter are the most important holidays in Hungary. Hungarians also celebrate Saint Nicholas Day on December 6. Children leave their shoes out the night before. In the morning, the shoes are filled with treats.

Fireworks light up the sky over Budapest on Saint Stephen's Day.

FACT!

Béla Bartók was one of Hungary's greatest **composers.** He blended traditional folk music with classical music.

Hungary celebrates its 1848 revolution against Austria on March 15. People listen to speeches and march in parades. August 20 is Saint Stephen's Day. This day honors Hungary's first king. There are always lots of fireworks!

Art is very important in Hungary. There are many art museums. Folk art is also popular. People enjoy painting flowers, birds, and plants on furniture, plates, and other objects.

Let's Dance!

Hungarian dance houses are found all over the country. There, people enjoy folk dances. Some dancers wear traditional costumes, including colorful skirts that spread out as dancers spin around.

People in Hungary enjoy many different sports. Soccer is the most popular. People also enjoy riding bikes. The country has almost 1,400 miles (2,200 kilometers) of trails. Other popular sports include hiking and horseback riding.

Visitors enjoy the Szechenyi Baths in Budapest.

Hungarians also enjoy water sports. They love to swim and play water polo. Kayaking and sailing are common too.

FACT!

Lake Balaton is a popular place. Many people enjoy swimming, boating, and fishing on this lake.

Olympic Glory

Hungarians have won gold medals at every Summer Olympics except two that they did not attend. Their best sports are fencing and swimming. Between 1896 and 2016, Hungarians won 175 gold medals.

Swimmer Katinka Hosszu after winning a gold medal in 2016

Hungarian families and friends enjoy spending time together. They visit museums and parks. They go out to eat and attend concerts, movies, and plays. There is always something fun to do in Hungary!

27

Food

Hungarian food is often very spicy! Paprika is a spice that is made in Hungary. It is used in many foods. For example, it is an important ingredient in a rich stew called goulash. Goulash is a mix of beef, potatoes, tomatoes, peppers, and onions.

Sausages and shish kebabs of grilled meat and vegetables are popular street foods.

FACT!

Langos is a popular street food. It is a fried dough that is topped with sour cream and cheese.

Sweet Treats

Kiffles are a popular cookie often eaten on holidays. These cookies are filled with fruit jam and topped with powdered sugar.

A *kiffle* filled with sweet apricot jam

Hungarians enjoy beef and chicken dishes. Meat is often served with noodles or dumplings. Cabbage leaves and peppers can be stuffed with meat or rice to create a filling and tasty meal.

Hungarians also like sweets. Pancakes called *palacsinta* are filled with fruit and nuts. Hungarians also enjoy cakes made of apples and walnuts.

Glossary

communist   A type of government where all property is owned by the state.

composers   People who write music.

ethnic   Related to people who have a common national or cultural tradition.

founder   Someone who starts a country.

persecuted   Treated unfairly because of ethnicity or religious beliefs.

republic   A government where power is held by the people.

trade   A job that requires special skills and training.

Find Out More

Books

Bjorklund, Ruth. *Hungary*. New York: Scholastic, 2016.

Esbenshade, Richard, and Debbie Nevins. *Cultures of the World: Hungary*. New York: Cavendish Square Publishing, 2016.

Website

Geography for Kids: Hungary

https://www.ducksters.com/geography/country.php?country=Hungary

Hungary Facts

https://kids.kiddle.co/Hungary

Video

10 Fun Facts About Hungary

https://www.youtube.com/watch?v=j8p67VP_rMk

Index

About the Author

Joanne Mattern is the author of more than 250 books for children. She specializes in nonfiction and has explored many different places in her writing. Her favorite topics include history, travel, sports, biography, and animals. Mattern lives in New York State with her husband, four children, and several pets.